W9-AWL-781

21st Century
Basic Skills
Library

WE CELEBRATE THANKSGIVING IN FALL

by Rebecca Felix

Cherry Lake Publishing • Ann Arbor, Michigan

Published in the United States of America
by Cherry Lake Publishing
Ann Arbor, Michigan
www.cherrylakepublishing.com

Consultant: Marla Conn, Read-Ability

Photo Credits: Courtney Weittenhiller/iStockphoto, cover, 1; Gord Horne/
iStockphoto, 4; iStockphoto, 6, 10, 12; Monkey Business Images/
Shutterstock Images, 8; Blend Images/Shutterstock Images, 14; Monkey
Business Images/Shutterstock Images, 16; Charles Sykes/AP Images, 18;
Shutterstock Images, 20

Library of Congress Cataloging-in-Publication Data
Felix, Rebecca, 1984-
  We celebrate Thanksgiving in fall / Rebecca Felix.
       p. cm. -- (Let's look at fall)
  Includes index.
  ISBN 978-1-61080-904-7 (hardback : alk. paper) -- ISBN 978-1-61080-
929-0 (paperback : alk. paper) -- ISBN 978-1-61080-954-2 (ebook) -- ISBN
978-1-61080-979-5 (hosted ebook)
 1. Thanksgiving Day--Juvenile literature. I. Title.

 GT4975.F45 2013
 394.2649--dc23

                                            2012030457

Cherry Lake Publishing would like to acknowledge
the work of The Partnership for 21st Century Skills.
Please visit www.21stcenturyskills.org for more information.

Printed in the United States of America
Corporate Graphics Inc.
January 2013
CLFA10

TABLE OF CONTENTS

What Do You See?

What farm machine do you see?

Fall Begins

Fall is here. It is a time of **harvest**.

Many foods become **ripe**. They are ready to pick. Tim picks vegetables.

Holiday

People give thanks for the food. This holiday is called Thanksgiving.

What Do You See?

What foods do you see?

10

Thanksgiving is in the month of November. People **prepare** a big feast.

Food

Sue helps cook a turkey. It is the main dish.

Jen helps bake an apple pie. She helps with the pumpkin pie, too.

Gather

Nick's family and friends gather. They give thanks. They eat together.

What animal do you see?

There is a Thanksgiving **parade** in New York. Many people watch it.

Fall Ends

Fall is over soon after Thanksgiving. What holiday comes next?

Find Out More

BOOK

Wing, Natasha. *The Night Before Thanksgiving*. New York: Grosset & Dunlap-Penguin, 2001.

WEB SITE

Thanksgiving Crafts—Enchanted Learning
www.enchantedlearning.com/crafts/thanksgiving
Find crafts, games, and quizzes about Thanksgiving.

Glossary

harvest (HAHR-vist) to gather crops

parade (puh-RADE) a show that moves along a street or area

prepare (prih-PAIR) to get ready

ripe (RIPE) full-grown and ready to be eaten

Home and School Connection

Use this list of words from the book to help your child become a better reader. Word games and writing activities can help beginning readers reinforce literacy skills.

animal	feast	month	ripe
apple	food	November	thanks
cook	friends	parade	Thanksgiving
dish	gather	people	together
eat	harvest	pick	turkey
fall	helps	pie	vegetables
family	holiday	prepare	
farm	machine	pumpkin	

What Do You See?

What Do You See? is a feature paired with select photos in this book. It encourages young readers to interact with visual images in order to build the ability to integrate content in various media formats.

You can help your child further evaluate photos in this book with additional activities. Look at the images in the book without the What Do You See? feature. Ask your child to describe one detail in each image, such as a food, activity, or setting.

Index

About the Author

Rebecca Felix is an editor and writer from Minnesota. She celebrates Thanksgiving with her family. She eats a lot of turkey and watches the Thanksgiving parade!